Priscilla Shirer

Breathe

making room for sabbath

Lifeway Press® Nashville, Tennessee

Published by Lifeway Press®

© 2014 Priscilla Shirer • Reprinted August 2021

ISBN 978-1-4300-3234-2

Item 005644896

Dewey decimal classification: 248.843

Subject headings: WOMEN \ STRESS (PSYCHOLOGY) \ REST

To order additional copies of this resource, write to Lifeway Resources, Customer Service, One Lifeway Plaza, Nashville, TN 37234-0113; fax 615.251.5933; phone 800.458.2772; order online at *www.lifeway.com* or email *orderentry@lifeway.com*.

Printed in the United States of America

Adult Ministry Publishing, Lifeway Resources, One Lifeway Plaza, Nashville, TN 37234-0152

DEDICATION

To Kay Arthur and Beth Moore,

For teaching me to say "No."

For inspiring me to put first things first.

For showing me by your example the importance of margin and Sabbath.

For reminding me that doing everything is not the same as doing the best things.

Thank you. You have taught me that life is better when it has room to breathe.

I love you.

Priscilla

PRISCILLA SHIRER

is a wife and mom first, but put a Bible in her hand and a message in her heart, and you'll see why thousands meet God in powerful, personal ways at her conferences.

With a master's degree in biblical studies from Dallas Theological Seminary, Priscilla brings the depths of Scripture to life. Her nine Bible studies span such topics as the exodus, hearing the voice of God, and biblical characters like Jonah and Gideon. She has also written seven books, including the New York Times bestseller *The Resolution for Women*.

Priscilla and her husband, Jerry, lead Going Beyond Ministries, through which they provide spiritual training, support, and resources to the body of Christ. They count it as their greatest privilege to serve every denomination and culture across the spectrum of the church.

CONTENTS

NOTE FROM PRISCILLA

We moved out to the country in search of simplicity. Jerry and I packed up our three boys, trading a neighborhood of concrete driveways and busy roads, for a more rural setting.

Our much smaller house sits on a sleepy two-lane road. All around us are cattle-filled green pastures instead of brick-clad buildings. Deep creeks replace carefully chiseled sidewalks. Neighbors are friends who wave on their quarter-mile walk up the driveway to the mailbox and then cross the lawn to come over and share sweet tea.

So naturally, seeing all this, I just thought a less complicated life would find us here automatically. I thought it would invite us to sit down in a rocking chair on the front porch and sway the day away under the spell of a cool breeze. I imagined that it would strip us of the need to buy too much, accumulate too much, say too much, or do too much. I assumed that our penchant for excess and busyness would magically wash away just because we moved ten minutes out of the suburbs.

It didn't. Turns out, a geographical move wasn't a suitable replacement for a mental and spiritual one. So, my house in the country soon begged for relief from overcrowded closets and drawers, just like the one in the city, and our family calendar pleaded for freedom from the load of far too many activities, same as before. It all found us right here.

All. Of. It.

That's what busyness and clutter do. They find you. Stalk you in the wee hours of the night. Keep you awake and uneasy. They corner you and demand more time, money, and energy than you have to offer. They coerce you into making bargains you can't hold up on your end. Then they leave you in a heap of exhaustion.

Tired. Overwhelmed. Dilapidated.

But if peace and contentment can't be found by moving to a quieter part of town, and if they can't be obtained by getting better organized, then what's the secret? Where can we find it?

Thankfully, the remedy has always been tucked in the well-worn pages of the Word. So I opened my Bible and took a brand new peek at an age-old principle—the Sabbath. The solution for the chaos was right here all along. I could have found and incorporated it just as well in the old house as I could in this new one. No moving truck required.

Now the Sabbath principle isn't necessarily easy to apply. I suspect that we'll always be a little resistant to it. So, like any good girlfriend, I want to forewarn you: this study journal is going to be difficult. We're sisters, so I feel like I have to spill the beans right up front. As I've taught and written this message, it has made me uncomfortable more than once. I'm not joking. And most of the time, the conviction doesn't stay confined to my heart, mind, and soul, but fills me with a sense of physical urgency to do something about it. Immediately.

This practical topic can't help but challenge you right away. I taught on it for the first time at the Deeper Still event in 2012. All ten thousand of us squirmed in our seats. The video in this study comes from that event, and the book will help you put feet to the message.

I'm asking you to sign up for the long haul—to refuse to go on with life as usual. I mean literally … sign up. You see that line under my signature? That's for your John Hancock. Sign your name once you've prayerfully agreed to go this distance with me. It's our commitment to each other to do serious business with God on this issue. Require yourself to answer the difficult questions, and make the life modifications that those answers dictate.

You can find room to breathe. We can do it together. It'll make wherever we live so much better. Ready? Let's go. Freedom waits on the other side of our obedience.

Priscilla Shirer

_____

YOUR SIGNATURE

7

THE FREEDOM OF
THE SABBATH

SABBATH SET UP

Harriet Tubman, the great emancipator of thousands of slaves in America, is quoted as saying "I freed thousands of slaves. I could have freed thousands more, if they had known they were slaves."[1]

If. Only. They. Knew.

Whoa. My eyes widened as I read this statement and realized its implications: Slavery is often the outcome of ignorance or denial; freedom hinges on recognition and acceptance.

BIG IDEA: Recognition is the prerequisite of liberation.

I want to confess right here at the beginning of our study: I was a slave and didn't know it. I was bound by things I never even thought of as possible taskmasters. They were good things God had given me full license to enjoy, yet they had begun to exert far too much control over my life. The very fact that my flesh cringed at the thought of curbing my desire to buy this or eat that, to spend time doing this and not that, should have been my first indicator that something was awry. My flesh was becoming enslaved to things it was meant to enjoy as blessings, not as bondage.

But I ignored the warnings and just carried on.

A captive unaware.

I have discovered, however—and am still discovering, after studying, reading, thinking, and praying about the Sabbath—that this one, beautiful biblical principle delivers freedom from a type of slavery I didn't even realize existed in my life. In the past, I'd thought of the Sabbath as nothing more than a day—a once-a-week, first-century observance dripping with too many rules and regulations to count, much less to observe. I discounted its relevance for me. Sabbath was so Old Testament, old-fashioned, old-school.

Little did I know that pulling back the layers of this Bible theme would shine a bright spotlight onto something always meant to be so much more than a rigid rule to follow, even when it was first established in Israel for a people who'd known nothing but slavery. God always and eternally intended the Sabbath to be a lifestyle—an attitude, a perspective, an orientation for living that enables us to govern our lives and steer clear of bondage.

Especially the bondages we are least likely to recognize . . .
- to things—like the stuff we buy: shoes, clothes, accessories, home décor, electronics
- to people—the boyfriend, the best friend, the employer
- to hobbies—golfing, watching television, reading, social media
- to indulgences—food, caffeine, chocolate
- to work—our jobs, ministries, careers, volunteer efforts.

I could go on, but somehow I feel like you can probably fill in the blank yourself. In fact, before we even really get started, I think you should.

Below write any things, people, interests, or endeavors that might just hold too much control over you right now in this season of your life. To what or whom do you find it difficult to say "no"?

Each of the following are good things. Some of them are even needful. But, depending on our unique personalities and interests, any of them could begin to control us if they aren't kept in check. Look at the list and consider how much of a danger each poses in your life.

Rate each of the following things on a scale from 1 (low danger) to 10 (extreme danger). Use the extra space on this page to record any thoughts that come to your mind about your relationship with any of these.

_____ shopping

_____ eating

_____ home decorating

_____ social media

_____ working

_____ ministry

_____ opinions of my friends

_____ opinions of people I don't even like

_____ marriage

_____ children

_____ relaxing

_____ hobbies

_____ exercise

_____ my weight

_____ my appearance

_____ sleep

_____ obsessing over something I've lost

_____ other _____

Together, you and I are going to find out how the Sabbath principle can keep these things from bossing us around, controlling our lives, and becoming masters over us. Sabbath margin is the boundary God intended for us to place around the things we enjoy so that we'll never be a slave to anyone or anything other than Him. He paid far too high a price for us to share our allegiance with any other. Jesus said,

> "You will know the truth, and the truth will set you free" (John 8:32).

Freedom from slavery begins with knowing. So let's get to it, shall we?

SESSION 1: VIEWER GUIDE

Are we so _____ with _____ that we can't even enjoy a break when it's thrust upon us?

We _____ the things we are _____ to.

Because anything we've been given to enjoy outside of the _____ in which it was designed to flourish will cause …

_____

_____

_____

_____

in our lives.

God's boundaries are _____.

In Deuteronomy 5:6-21, Moses reviews the 10 _____.

The Sabbath was a _____.

Word for Sabbath in Hebrew is _____, it means

to _____, to _____, to _____,

to come to _____.

The Sabbath was a _____ against the children of Israel

becoming _____ again.

SESSION 1: GROUP QUESTIONS

✶ If you'd been interviewed for the newspaper article, how would you have responded to the reporter's question?

✶ Did any good gifts that have begun to have too much control over you come to mind while you were listening?

✶ How do you see evidence that these things or people have too much control in your life?

✶ How do you normally respond to the boundaries your friends establish in their lives? Do you support the boundaries or find yourself being frustrated with them?

✶ God gave the Sabbath to Israel as a gift for which they should have been grateful. In what ways does the thought of having margin and boundaries in your life feel like a gift from God? In what ways does it feel like bondage?

Video sessions available for purchase at *www.lifeway.com/breathe*

WEEK 1: AND HE RESTED ...

THIS WEEK'S BIG IDEA:
The Sabbath principle is the key to freedom.

The word "Sabbath" first appears in Scripture during the exodus from Egypt. But that's not the first time the concept is mentioned. Take note of Genesis 2.

> "By the seventh day God completed His work that He had done, and He rested on the seventh day from all His work that He had done (Gen. 2:2)."

Obviously, God had the Sabbath in mind from the very beginning.

Abraham Joshua Heschel, a twentieth-century Jewish rabbi and author, wrote something I find profound about this Genesis 2 passage in his book *The Sabbath: Its Meaning for Modern Man*. Read the following excerpt slowly, and pay close attention to the portions I've highlighted. Note the word *menuha* means *rest* in Hebrew.

> "The words: 'On the seventh day God finished His work' (Genesis 2:2), seem to be a puzzle. . . .We would surely expect the Bible to tell us that on the sixth day God finished His work. Obviously, the ancient rabbis concluded, there was an act of creation on the seventh day. Just as heaven and earth were created in six days, menuha was created on the Sabbath. After the six days of creation—what did the universe still lack? *Menuha*. Came the Sabbath, came menuha, and the universe was complete."[2]

Before we continue with Rabbi Heschel's statement, take a moment to re-read the highlighted portions of the quote. Take your time. I'll wait.

Record your observations and insights about the highlighted portions of the quote.

Heschel continues:

> "Menuha, which we usually render with "rest" means here much more than withdrawal from labor and exertion, more than freedom from toil, strain or activity of any kind. Menuha is not a negative concept but something real and intrinsically positive. This must have been the view of the ancient rabbis if they believed that it took a special act of creation to bring it into being, that the universe would be incomplete without it. 'What was created on the seventh day? Tranquility, serenity, peace and repose.'"[3]

All right, I'll wait for you to read the highlighted sections here again as well. Remember, S.L.O.W.L.Y. Drink it in.

Record your thoughts about the highlighted portions.

I'm so intrigued by this. The purpose of God's Sabbath day was not to put up His proverbial feet, take a load off, and chill out after creating the universe in the previous days. Turns out, He wasn't doing just nothing. Far from it. He was creating something.

Rest.

Rest was the capstone of creation and without it the universe would be incomplete.

Given the insights from what you've just read, how is the concept of rest more than simply stopping an activity? How is rest a positive, created thing rather than a negative cessation of activity?

Think of how you would teach this idea to a younger believer or one of your children. How might you help that person understand that rest is a real, tangible thing that is worth creating in our lives?

Heschel said that on the seventh day God created "tranquility, serenity, peace, and repose."

To give you an opportunity to think even more deeply about what God created here, choose one or more of those four terms, and search for their definitions online or in your dictionary. Record any interesting defining words below.

Recall and describe a time when you saw "tranquility, serenity, peace, and repose" created in your life as a result of placing Sabbath margin in each of the following:

✱ work schedule:

✱ family schedule:

✱ hobbies:

✱ appetites:

✱ another area of your life:

Why do you think we tend to view Sabbath space and margin from a negative perspective (stopping something) instead of from God's positive perspective (creating something)?

Consider the areas of your life that you rated the highest in the exercise at the beginning of this chapter (p. 11) and write them below. For each, how do you need to see "tranquility, serenity, peace, and repose" created and experienced?

Brad Lomenick, respected innovator and leader of the Catalyst Movement in America, writes:

> "Margin is a powerful concept. It creates *opportunities*. For businesses, margin is one of your top priorities. Margin in business creates profits. Margin in family creates memories. Margin in our personal finances creates generosity. Margin in our friendships creates significance and impact. Margin in our lives overall creates *options*. Options to pursue dreams, think, pray, relax, meditate, process, grow and ultimately live life more fully."[4]

Perpetual Motion

Let me begin this segment by clearly stating: I'm no scientist. In fact, when God was handing out the brain wiring for math and science, I was standing in the wrong line. But I do remember from my high school chemistry class that everything is made of atoms and subatomic particles. At the atomic and subatomic level, everything in creation is constantly in motion. The chair you're seated in right now seems to be "sitting" still, doesn't it? But it's not. It's actually buzzing with activity. The protons and electrons that circle the nuclei in the atoms never stop moving. Never. We cannot make them stop.

Sounds so much like us, huh? Even when we look like we're resting, our minds are still buzzing. Or at the very least, our cell phones are. And few of us do very well turning either one of them off.

That's why God's practice, and later His institution, of Sabbath is such a countercultural act. In the midst of a universe that cannot exist for a second without constant motion, God transcended the order of nature. He stopped. He rested. And He prescribes the same for you and me. It is actually one of the ways that the image of God shows itself in our lives when we stop in a constantly moving world.

{ Theologians use the word *transcendence* to describe what is infinitely removed from mankind. It is an experience beyond the normal or physical level. Sabbath rest could be the ultimate transcendence. }

Using those insights, describe how the Sabbath principle counters the foundational experience of the physical world.

When we neglect time to create "tranquility, serenity, peace, and repose" in our lives, we limit our Christlikeness and miss out on some of God's greatest gifts. Not only that, but in the words of Jeremiah 25:7, we actually "provoke" God to anger and bring "harm" on ourselves (NASB).

Think back, again, to those areas you rated highest in your life. In what ways have you experienced difficulty or harm as a result of rejecting God's command to stop and practice tranquility?

We are going to look at this in more detail during the final week of our study but for now, consider the implications of the fact that God Himself practiced the Sabbath principle long before He ever expected it from His people. This is God's way—teaching by example and by precept. He shows us truth, then He teaches us truth. So before He ever taught the principle overtly, He demonstrated it personally.

Why do you suppose God practiced the principle of a seventh day rest, long before He instructed His children to observe the day?

I was discussing with several friends why implementing the Sabbath principle is so difficult for us. We agreed on one of the reasons we often feel guilty or embarrassed when we establish margin and boundaries in our lives or our family's lives. We're concerned that others will classify us as lazy. Several mothers admitted they feel the need to keep up with the schedule of their friends' children. They often feel snubbed by other parents if their child isn't involved in, you know . . . everything.

Somehow our culture has caused us to believe that busier is better. We've become unknowingly convinced that taking time to create rest and tranquility means we are unfit, weak, or incompetent. We've rejected the art of saying "no" without guilt or regret. We've fallen prey to the myth that if we don't have as much or don't do as much as others, then we're somehow not as valuable.

But wait . . .

Knowing that God Almighty, Maker of heaven and earth, valued Sabbath enough Himself to practice it as a key aspect of Creation . . . doesn't this seriously challenge the mind-set that rest is only for wimps and weaklings? God certainly isn't a wimp. He also has never been lazy, embarrassed, ashamed, or feeble for having margin.

Do you ever fear being perceived as weak or lazy? Do you struggle with a sense of guilt for creating margin in your schedule? Explain.

How does the fact that your omnipotent God took a Sabbath rest quell your concern?

Do you ever have anxiety about not fitting in with others if you don't have as much as they do? What effect does this have on your self-esteem?

What effect does this anxiety have on your relationship with others?

We can easily agree with all of this on paper can't we? We know deep down inside that a life filled to the brim and spilling over—congested and smothered—isn't the way it's supposed to be. Yet despite this knowing, and despite the foundational example God provided for us in the very first pages of the Bible, we still tend to believe our way is better. We think we are the exception to the rule, and that we don't need Sabbath space. Or perhaps we just don't think we can afford the margin. But when you dig a little deeper into our reasons for keeping our lives so full, busy, and crammed with more than we can successfully manage, maybe there's more to it than we'd like to admit.

What are the deep-seated reasons why we tend to think that busier/fuller lives are better? See if any of the following statements strike close to home for you. Jot your thoughts after each statement.

- A full life brings us a sense of significance, security, or worth. We use busyness and overindulgence as a means of self-exaltation.

- We do not trust God to fulfill His promises to us, so we play God, falsely believing we need to provide, finish, do, control, and hoard.

- We place our hope and joy in things that ultimately do not fulfill.

- We fear what others will think or say if we aren't keeping pace with everyone else or don't seem to be keeping up with the "Joneses."

- We don't know how to be still. We never learned.

- We don't know how to be content and satisfied. We never learned.

- We don't like ourselves enough to be alone with ourselves for an extended period of time.

Circle any of the above reasons that apply to you.

Record below any other reasons that come to mind.

Remember from our video session, that the Sabbath principle is not limited to our calendars and schedules. It also applies to the spaces in which we live, work and play. Our tendency toward too-full lives often expresses itself most tangibly in our over-crowded closets, unmanageable table surfaces and cluttered desks as we cram them full of far more than we need. Even our children fall prey to the chaos of overcrowded living as their toy boxes and bookshelves overflow with more than they could ever manage. In the meantime they sit, chin in hand, complaining of boredom.

If you haven't already, turn your attention from busyness to over-accumulating and hoarding. Why do you think we humans have a tendency to accrue massive amounts of things? What keeps us from stopping?

In what ways have you found that accumulated things do not deliver the happiness that they seem to promise?

Sabbath, Slavery, and Snowstorms

Let's move forward now from Genesis 1 to the time period when God first introduced the Sabbath principle directly to Israel—after their release from Egypt.

The Israelites had lived in slavery so long that their inclination—even once outside of Egypt—was to live like they were still in bondage. They had become accustomed to enslavement as a lifestyle. It was all they'd ever known. They had internalized the demands to always be working, doing, producing, and performing, never allowed to say "no" and refuse the demands of their taskmasters. Being dominated and restrained by someone else—controlled, compelled, commanded— was their normal experience.

And God, of course, knew. He knew that even with freedom as an everyday reality, they would always revert to bondage of some sort. Strangely, slavery had become comfortable for them, enough that they were no longer capable of unassisted freedom. The reality is—for

#sabbathmargin

them and for us—that once slavery has been internalized, the mind remains in bondage even when the body is free. Without an experience of rest, the concept of margin, breathing room, and boundary is difficult for someone with a slave mentality to understand.

So, God prescribed for His people—then and now—a loving, gracious gift that would break the chains that remained inside of them. The gift was called Sabbath.

He knew, for them to be truly free, He would need to do more than just take them out of Egypt; He also needed to take the Egypt out of them. The very essence of the Sabbath principle—to cease, stop striving, and trust—went completely against their nature, making it extremely difficult for them to incorporate into their mind-sets. But to experience freedom, they needed to practice the discipline of freedom. A change in their hearts would be the result of practical changes in their lifestyle. The Sabbath was one of the main remedies Yahweh employed to assist in the freedom of their souls.

In what ways do you think we can be freed from the curse of sin yet still possess a slave mentality as we journey through life?

Are you seeing this reality play out in some specific way in your life right now? If so, how?

The very first time the term "Sabbath" actually appears in Scripture is Exodus 16:23, when Moses told God's people, "This is what the LORD has said: 'Tomorrow is a day of complete rest, a holy Sabbath to the LORD.'"

Place yourself in the worn sandals of the escaping Israelite slaves. How do you think you would have received the command to take a day of rest?

- "Wow. I'm delighted."

- "What will others think of me if I'm unproductive?"

- Confused: "Who ever heard of such a thing?"

- "What if I get behind on my work?"

- I'm afraid my family and I won't have enough if I take time off.

- Some other response?

> "Can you imagine what the gift of the sabbath meant to the Israelites standing at the foot of Mount Sinai? A few months prior they had been slaves. ... Slaves whose **only value** was the quantity of labor they could produce before their backs gave way and their strength failed. Slaves who, outside of a holy day or two, worked every day of their lives—from the tenderest days of their childhood until their broken bodies were laid in the ground. And now this God, who has claimed them as his 'treasured possession,' is announcing that one day out of every seven will be set apart for rest."[5]

The original Sabbath command specified a whole day of complete rest. We will explore the specifics of this application as we go along, but let me ask you a question based on this Exodus passage alone:

In our modern culture, how have you seen that we have turned a day of rest from a blessing into an arduous burden?

In the video segment this week, I told the story about the snowstorm in my hometown and people's negative reaction to taking a mandatory break from the regular rhythms of living. Some took the snowstorm as the gift of a much-needed break from lives that were stretched at the seams with too much activity. Others, however, felt the same event was almost like a punishment.

What does the fact that people viewed rest as a burden say about their view of busyness?

What does it say about their view of margin?

Why do you think one is valued above the other?

Freedom Works

One of my life verses is Galatians 5:1. It's been one of my favorites since my days as an undergraduate student at the University of Houston.

> "For freedom Christ has set us free; stand firm therefore, and do not submit again to a yoke of slavery" (Gal. 5:1, ESV).

God gave us freedom as a gift. But living free requires a firm resolve to continue walking in it, resisting the attempts of this world and our Enemy to put chains back onto us again. We must be deliberate and intentional about setting guardrails around our endeavors so that we can travel freely to the places God is taking us, staying on the main road the whole way.

What do those guardrails need to look like? What boundaries will do the best job of keeping distraction and dysfunction out, while they keep freedom and fullness in? Many of our problems can be resolved if we simply take the time and energy to write down our priorities and parameters, and then filter every opportunity through them.

BIG IDEA: Parameters keep things in place.

Since Jerry and I work together in ministry, for example, we're forced to be extra cautious about keeping conversations and endeavors that relate to our ministry life from spilling over into those hours that should be reserved for enhancing our relationship and family. We certainly aren't perfect at this, and will probably struggle to maintain balance for as long as the Lord allows us to do what we do. But to guard against it, we intentionally mark specific days and hours onto our calendar that are reserved just for "us." These are our guardrails.

Let's go back up to the things you listed on page 10 as areas you may be prone to overdo.

List them again here.

Now prayerfully record as many practical guardrails as possible that can help you stand firm and maintain your freedom in these areas.

Which of these parameters do you think will be most difficult for you to adhere to?

Who can you enlist as accountability?

As incentive for your new endeavors, record the ways that your commitment to the Sabbath principle will enrich your life by creating tranquility and peace and help maintain your freedom in Christ.

As I've previously stated, God instituted principles, themes, and laws that would transform the Israelites' mind-set. He didn't just want them legally free. He wanted them to be able to walk in their freedom and enjoy it. So God gave them many gifts, but He also gave them boundaries in which to enjoy those gifts. Those boundaries were gifts as well.

BIG IDEA: Boundaries are not burdens. They are gifts.

Underline the last sentence in the previous paragraph.

Why do you suppose we so seldom recognize boundaries as gifts?

Years ago a sociologist conducted a study to determine the benefits and disadvantages of boundaries. You may remember it. The experts put a group of children on a playground with no railing or fence, telling them to go enjoy themselves. But instead of roaming the full breadth of the yard, the children stayed fairly close by. It appeared that since they were uncertain of how far was too far they opted for security and didn't explore the full range of the space. During the next experiment, the sociologist put the children in a playground enclosed by a sturdy fence line. When the children were set loose to play this time, they explored every crevice and inch of the property—roaming the full range of their playground on all sides. They went further and enjoyed more when they had boundaries than when they didn't.

The boundary released them to enjoy the whole space they'd been given access to.

Can you think of another illustration you can use to describe how boundaries enhance the gifts God gives to us?

During the video message, I used an illustration of a fire in a fireplace. Using a different illustration, how would you explain to a 10-year-old child the idea that anything we've been given to enjoy, outside of the boundaries in which it was designed to flourish, will cause chaos, catastrophe, and disaster in our lives?

How do you think we can cultivate a greater appreciation for the boundaries God has given us?

If you are a parent, what do you think you can do to cultivate an appreciation for boundaries in your children?

The Sabbath day was both an opportunity for the children of Israel to have some margin that would enhance their enjoyment of their new life and an exercise in showing a heightened respect for Yahweh. But they didn't appreciate the gift. Israel likely felt about the same as we do about taking a space of time to simply appreciate God.

By the time of the New Testament, it got worse. The religious leaders attached so many regulations and requirements to the law that it squeezed out the purpose for which God had given the gift in the first place. Today, if we aren't careful, we'll also be unable to realize and appreciate the beauty of God's intention.

Hebrews 4 says a "rest" remains for the people of God and that we have to "make every effort to enter that rest, so that no one will fall into the same pattern of disobedience" (v. 11).

Don't miss these three important words: Make. Every. Effort.

Listen, the journey ahead of us in this study and in our lives is going to require an "effort." Discipline and diligence will always be prerequisites if we expect to experience the freedom and rest that God intends for us. To dive deeply into this concept, and then to align our decisions and lifestyle patterns to the truths we uncover, will be no walk in the park. But as a girl who's watching this Sabbath principle unshackle the chains from my life, more and more every day, I can tell you it's worth all the effort we expend.

So don't wait, OK? Let's start today, setting some strategic boundaries around the things, people, habits, or activities that we are most prone to become enslaved to and controlled by.

Freedom lies on the other side of our obedience.

I hope this has been an eye-opening week of prayerful study for you. It certainly has been for me. I'm looking forward to next week already.

YOUR BIG IDEAS …

At the end of each week, there will be a section like this one called "YOUR BIG IDEAS". This is your opportunity to record your personal takeaways and insights. What has God taught you? What have you been most surprised to discover about yourself or the concept we are studying? What are your intentions and plans to apply what you have been studying?

You've noticed that I've scattered my "Big Ideas" throughout the study and I've even used the #sabbathmargin hashtag. This is for those of you who are twitter or instagram users and want to tweet these Big Ideas or others that God gives you. Using our #sabbathmargin hashtag will give us a chance to stay connected. Women from Bible study groups everywhere will be able to find your tweets and to be encouraged by what God is teaching through this study.

_____

_____

_____

_____

_____

_____

_____

_____

_____

_____

_____

_____

_____

I want to leave you with a couple of quotes/sayings that I've run into recently. See if the Lord uses any of them to speak to you specifically.

> "Some of us have made an idol of exhaustion. The only time we know we have done enough is when we're running on empty and when the ones we love most are the ones we see the least." —Barbara Brown Taylor[6]

> "Sabbath-keeping: Quieting the internal noise so we hear the still small voice of the Lord. Removing the distractions of pride so we discern the presence of Christ."
> —Eugene Peterson[7]

WEEK 2

STOPS ALONG THE SABBATH JOURNEY

SABBATH SET UP

My senior year in high school ended with a trip to London—a gift from my parents and Aunt Ruth who has lived there her entire adult life. Together, a friend and I arrived in England for a week of exploration.

You'd think we'd have taken the opportunity to visit historic sites, tour the royal residences, and glean fascinating information from museums. But we were teenagers, uninterested in such official tour-guided things. We wanted nothing more than just to watch movies and walk the streets aimlessly for hours at a time, ducking into little boutiques and candy shops.

We didn't have much money, just enough to catch the bus to and from my aunt's home, then buy a ticket to see a film at the theatre in Piccadilly Circus. After one of those movies, we walked into the donut shop across the street (as if we needed more sugar) and ordered our favorite chocolate-filled, glazed sweets.

I walked up to the register while fishing around in my purse for a few dollars to pay. But as I pulled out my wallet and looked inside, I was shocked. There was no money in it. The dollars we had exchanged for British pounds earlier in the day were missing.

Assuming they had merely fallen out into my purse, I kept digging and searching—in and out of pockets, deep into the bottom of my bag. Nothing.

My friend, conscious of the line forming behind us, jumped to the front in a heroic attempt to save me from embarrassment, "Don't worry. I'll take care of it." She reached into her purse and pulled out her wallet, only to make her own shocking discovery as well.

Her money was missing, too.

We'd been robbed.

Apparently, while we were engrossed in the movie, the sneaky thieves had lain down on the floor behind our row in the darkened theater and quietly pulled our bags from beside our feet.

Then, as if to mock us even more, they'd removed our wallets, taken out the cash, returned the wallets to their proper place, and pushed the purses back to their positions beside us. They knew they'd be halfway home before we even became aware of what they had done.

*   If only we'd kept our bags in our laps instead of on the floor.

*   If only we'd held them close to us instead of taking our hands and eyes off of them.

*   If only we had kept them under our control.

Maybe this robbery would never have happened.

We—you and I—have fallen victim to a far worse theft. Hoodwinked. Bamboozled. We've been pickpocketed by a sinister culprit who slipped a sense of peace and joy right out of our lives—gifts reserved and fully intended for all of God's children.

Worse, we often don't even know our peace and joy are missing until one day when everything begins to unravel, and we're stressed out, frustrated, and overwhelmed. We reach down into our internal reserves to pull out the deep-rooted characteristics we need for sustaining life through the difficult places, and we're shocked to find that we're running on empty, with nothing to sustain us for the long haul.

The currency we need for living life well has been stolen right out from under our noses.

If only we can take back the reins, regain control, and get the things we value off the floor and back into the center of our attention. Maybe then we won't be such an easy target for the Enemy who lurks nearby, ready and waiting to rob us blind.

This week, we're going to look closely at the first key to making that happen—to regaining control and staving off our Adversary. And I think we'll get back much of what's been stolen from us as an added bonus along the way.

SESSION 2: VIEWER GUIDE

They had never been told _____ _____ _____

SABBATH PRINCIPLES

I. Resist the urge to _____.

Two Boundaries for Receiving Manna:

1. Gather every day for six days, but on the _____ don't

   _____.

2. Gather enough for each day; do not _____ _____ for
   the _____ _____.

SESSION 2: GROUP QUESTIONS

✳ The Israelites were told to resist the urge to work because, as a people group, work was their specific compulsion. Other than work, what do you see as the main obsessions of the people in your sphere of influence?

✳ What are the positives and negatives of the technological age? How is the broadening of technology supporting workaholism?

✳ Resisting the flesh is the key to spiritual victory. Consider Galatians 5:16-23 and discuss what it looks like to be led by the Spirit.

✳ What are practical ways to resist the flesh?

✳ In what ways do you most clearly see that the enjoyment of life is being squeezed out by excess?

Video sessions available for purchase at *www.lifeway.com/breathe*

WEEK 2: COMING TO A FULL STOP

THIS WEEK'S BIG IDEA: Just say no.

Underline the three actions listed at the end of the following definition.

> *Shabbat*—the Hebrew word for Sabbath—means "to come to an end, to cease, to stop, to pause."

Notice they are all active commands that a person needs to take responsibility for. Something they have to do. To experience Sabbath margin, you must make a decision to stop something, to push away from something, to rest from something.

You have to say "no" to something.

Experiencing Sabbath space in our lives is contingent upon our ability to regain the self-control and inner strength required to deny both ourselves and other people at times and in certain situations.

Is the word "no" difficult for you to say to yourself? If so, in what areas?

Is it difficult for you to say "no" to others when they're pressuring you to do something? Why or why not?

The Ten Commandments appear twice in the Old Testament: once in Exodus and once in Deuteronomy. The 40 years of wilderness wandering took place between these two accounts.

Take a look at how the Sabbath command is communicated in both instances and see if you can detect the major difference between them.

"Remember the Sabbath day, to keep it holy: You are to labor six days and do all your work, but the seventh day is a Sabbath to the LORD your God. You must not do any work—you, your son or daughter, your male or female slave, your livestock, or the foreigner who is within your gates. For the LORD made the heavens and the earth, the sea, and everything in them in six days; then He rested on the seventh day. Therefore the LORD blessed the Sabbath day and declared it holy" (Ex. 20:8–11).

"Be careful to remember the Sabbath day, to keep it holy as the LORD your God has commanded you. You are to labor six days and do all your work, but the seventh day is a Sabbath to the LORD your God. You must not do any work—you, your son or daughter, your male or female slave, your ox or donkey, any of your livestock, or the foreigner who lives within your gates, so that your male and female slaves may rest as you do. Remember that you were a slave in the land of Egypt, and the LORD your God brought you out of there with a strong hand and an outstretched arm. That is why the LORD your God has commanded you to keep the Sabbath day" (Deut. 5:12-15).

Did you see it? You really have to concentrate to find it. I'll give you a hint: it's in the last two sentences of each of the paragraphs. Each passage notes a unique basis for Israel's adherence to the Sabbath.

Read it again and underline or highlight the difference.

Describe the difference in your own words.

In Exodus, the Sabbath commandment finds its foundation in the creation story, in God's resting on the seventh day. But when Moses recounts it for the Hebrews in Deuteronomy, he roots it firmly in their emancipation from slavery. The first is about Eden, but the second is all about Egypt.

Back in Egypt, the slaves of Israel had never been told not to work. Reprieve was a foreign concept to their culture. They had never been given the privilege to stop and rest, and had certainly never been given the option to decline a command given by their superiors. The Israelites had never developed the discipline of declining. They had been trained to always acquiesce and comply. But now, the Sabbath would help them remember they were free. Free to say "no." Free to rest. Free to no longer be controlled by that which they were previously mastered. Free to enjoy their relationship with Yahweh.

BIG IDEA: It takes discipline to decline.

Our situation isn't really all that different than Israel's. Like them, our flesh has not been trained to decline itself or to decline others. Our own impulses, combined with those of our culture, press us toward excess, leaving us weak-willed, our self-restraint flimsy. In actuality, our "freedom" has been a disguise—a feeble veneer—masking a new kind of slavery.

You read the following verse last week, but I want you to consider it again in a different translation. Prayerfully record how God's Spirit speaks to you through it:

> "In [this] freedom Christ has made us free [and completely liberated us]; stand fast then, and do not be hampered *and* held ensnared *and* submit again to a yoke of slavery [which you have once put off] (Gal. 5:1, AMP).

What new insights do you glean from this version?

Learning to Say "No"

Our inability to decline—to say "no"—has become legendary. A simple Web search yielded about a million hits including numerous articles giving advice on how to get better at saying "no."

A million—1,000,000! (Look at all those zeros).

Our lives must be quite out of balance to warrant so many recommendations from experts trying to tell us how to "stop the madness."

Those who minister in the area of addiction sometimes quote the old F. Scott Fitzgerald adage: "First you take a drink, then the drink takes a drink, then the drink takes you." Like a snowball gaining speed and girth with every turn, addicts of all sorts cross an invisible line, beyond which they give up the ability to effectively or confidently say "no." All too soon they've become flattened, run over by something that was once only a hobby.

But if they're ever to recover—if the snowball is ever to be slowed and thawed away—they must pick up this ability again: the discipline to decline. The Sabbath principle is one of the key rays of golden sunlight that can melt the snowball and keep it from running roughshod over them (and us) again. And again. And again.

So let's explore this foundational principle of Sabbath mentioned in our video session: resist the urge to continue. It was one of the benefits of freedom that God wanted His people to recognize and utilize, both then … and now.

What does the word *resist* imply about the relationship between two things?

What about the term *urge?*

Complete the following sentence: "I have a difficult time resisting the urge to continue . . ."

What makes it so difficult for you to stop?

"No" represents one of life's most basic and necessary boundaries. It keeps things, hobbies, work, and relationships in their proper place, and serves as a constant reminder of their position in your life. Honoring Sabbath margin by saying "no" when appropriate means you only have one God and your allegiance is to Him, not to your desire for *that* or *it* or *them*.

It—whatever your "it" is—isn't your god. God is. Once something is allowed to creep past its appropriate place in your life—once you're unable to say "no" to it—it has become an illegitimate god. It has become, according to Colossians 3:5, "idolatry."

What activity or intrusion have you needed to say "no" to in the past twenty-four hours?

What about in the past twenty minutes?

When God created the first couple (Adam and Eve), He instructed them, "You are free to eat from any tree of the garden, but you must not eat from the tree of the knowledge of good and evil, for on the day you eat from it, you will certainly die" (Gen. 2:16-17). Inherent in this command was the recognition of their ability to say "no." God had instilled in His highest creation the strength they needed to honor what He commanded.

They *could* resist and choose to honor God.

They *could* say "no" to the serpent's temptation.

They could keep from pushing God off the throne of their hearts and assuming the spot for themselves. All they needed to do was to access and exercise their privilege: the liberty of saying "no." This was freedom in its purest form—people making decisions that honor God without being bullied into sin by illegitimate desire.

Stop for a moment and re-read the highlighted sentence in the paragraph above. How did the first couple's actions displace God?

What does our inability to say "no" reveal about God's position in our lives?

What does your inability to say "no" reveal about your relationship with that substance, object, or person?

Adam and Eve's choice not to utilize the discipline that was instilled in their humanity robbed them of a profound possibility from that day forward. Sinlessness became a lost option. Rebellion was now let loose to swarm the flesh of mankind. As a result, from then until now, utilizing the discipline to decline has been an intense struggle for humans.

And yet . . .

For those of us who are believers in Christ Jesus it is possible. The Spirit of God lives in us, not only to enliven us, but also to empower us to regain control. We need only to surrender to His work in our lives. Yes, that's right. The Sabbath is about surrender. To the extent that you and

I yield to the Spirit's control, that's the extent to which we will begin to see His fruit flourish in our lives. He will empower us to be self-controlled and have the courage to say "no" without guilt, shame, or worry.

BIG IDEA: The Sabbath is about surrender.

Consider the spiritual fruit of self-discipline (see Gal. 5:17) in connection with saying "no." Record any correlation you detect.

In your own words, rewrite and expand on this idea:
The Sabbath is about surrender.

Enough Is Enough

Exodus 1 describes Israel's captors as taskmasters who were intent on afflicting them with brutality. The slaves were constantly in a position of trying to earn their approval and steer clear of this cruelty. Since they had been trained to appease their ruthless overlords in order to gain approval, this new Sabbath concept would be difficult to understand. If they weren't constantly working and producing, how could this new Master, Yahweh, love them the way He claimed?

Commanding the people to take a Sabbath was Yahweh's way of showing these newly freed people that their relationship with Him was not based on what they could do for Him. He loved them simply because they were His. He had chosen them. That was enough.

Take a moment to think deeply. Do you, in any way, feel that your value is tied up in accumulating more or in gaining approval through your performance?

If so, how does it make you feel about yourself when you continue striving?

How do you feel about yourself when you stop?

What areas of your life are you no longer enjoying because they're so overcrowded?

I slumped down into my sofa yesterday, remote in hand, mindlessly flipping channels. Exhausted from a long day, I just wanted to find something "easy" to watch that would lull me into a relaxing evening. But my scanning stopped when I came across the image of someone's kitchen completely overrun with dishes, dirt, old food, pots and pans, unopened boxes, and cat litter. I couldn't believe what I was seeing. The debris was piled so high on the kitchen floor that the homeowner literally had to use her hands to climb up and over it to get from the door to the kitchen sink—a sink that was nearly invisible because it was chock full of anything and everything. Cans of food with "use-by" dates extending back nearly a decade were scattered across the dusty countertops, along with plates caked with molded food, piled high, one on top of the other.

I was slack-jawed. How gross. And, to make matters worse, her kitchen wasn't the only room that had deteriorated to this horrific state. Her entire house was disastrous enough that the city had threatened to evict her if she didn't clean it up.

In the midst of all of the mayhem, the cameras caught sight of little porcelain faces peering out from crevices in the pile. This woman, turns out, was a doll collector. She had started with only one or two acquisitions, purchased every now and then on the Internet. But soon, unable to resist any purchasing opportunity, she'd accumulated thousands of them. Eventually, she'd neglected her home altogether in order to find space for her inanimate friends.

Tears ran down her face as she realized what a mess she was in. What had started out as just a hobby—collecting dolls—had turned into a tragic scenario that had alienated her loved ones and ruined her whole life.

I want you to picture the area of your life where this study most strikes a chord. It might not be the accumulation of things (at least not to the extent that you qualify for being profiled on the reality show *Hoarders*), but it could be any number of areas where you've lost a little control.

What in your life would equate to the kitchen or bedroom, the office or closet, the mind or heart of the person I saw on TV, where you're overrun with something, or someone, that's begun to take too much ground in your life? Got it firmly in your mind?

Take a deep breath, and say the following sentence three times out loud, both to yourself and to the Lord. Three times. Out loud. Ready?

"ENOUGH is ENOUGH!"

I'm serious. Say it out loud. Come on. Right now. Let's hear it.

It's OK. I'm saying it, too.

"Enough is enough . . . is enough . . . is enough."

It really is, Sister. It really is.

Now, spend some time asking the Lord to give you a holy courage and supernatural power to resist the urge to continue—to let enough be enough.

Take a moment to write down a strategy to help you in this area. What can you start doing immediately that will help you achieve slow and steady success?

Who can you enlist for accountability?

Leviticus says:

{ "It will be a Sabbath of complete rest for you, and you must practice self-denial" (Lev. 23:32). }

The Old Testament frequently links Sabbath and self-denial.

In what sense must you practice self-denial in order to achieve rest?

How is self-denial involved when you choose a better desire over a lesser desire?

How would self-denial have been a great gift to the woman on the TV show?

In a blog concerning self-denial, James Chastek writes:

> "The abandonment and forgetfulness of self-denial is so universal and has such profound effects ... Nothing so important has been so completely forgotten."[1]

Chastek draws these conclusions:

> "A Christianity that asks us to give nothing up is gotten cheaply, and is therefore treated like any other cheap thing. ... Consumption makes for dullness of mind and an alienation from spiritual things."[2]

What insights do you take from Chastek's blog post?

Do you agree that our constant desires contribute to making us unhappy? Explain.

If so, how might a disciplined Sabbath margin have the opposite effect. How might it make a difference in our quality of life?

I want to share one caution here. As we begin to institute godly parameters in our lives, our Enemy will seek to pervert these rightly intended guidelines until they are skewed to ridiculous proportions. He'll work hard to make them rigid rules that slice away at the joy that the Sabbath was intended to infuse into our lives. He'll try to reduce this whole venture to a set of mindless, legalistic mechanics that require nothing of our hearts' cooperation and take our eyes off of the main purpose.

Take a look at John 5:

> "This is why the Jews began trying all the more to kill Him: Not only was He breaking the Sabbath, but He was even calling God His own Father, making Himself equal with God" (John 5:18).

This passage illustrates the danger of legalism. The Pharisees determined to kill the Prince of peace for two reasons. First, because Jesus claimed to be equal to God the Father (an absolutely accurate allegation), and secondly, because they said He was breaking the Sabbath. Listen: they planned to sacrifice the Lamb of God on the altar of their man-made list of regulations. They had elevated the day above the Creator of that day.

This is the essence of legalism.

In your own words, describe *legalism.*

So as we draw our careful Sabbath guidelines, we have to be cautious about turning them into legalistic hoops that focus more on what we're giving up than on the freedom of what God is allowing us to enjoy. We have to be vigilant against being merely "rule-followers"—pious legalists who feel justified in casting judgment on others. Because, sadly, it's really simple—to stroke our egos through legalism; to feel just a little more holy than everyone else; to become as imprisoned by pride and discontentment as we were before by overcommitment and codependency.

Yes, sometimes even self-denial can become dangerous. Consider anorexia, for example—abstaining to the point of unhealthiness. While not always the case, certain forms of restriction like this can become just another expression of selfishness and indulgence.

As food for thought, record any ways that self-denial could morph into something unhealthy?

You and I should appropriately deny our flesh when we feel ourselves beginning to spin out of control. But rather than do so out of competitiveness, fear, or guilt, our decisions should be based on what one author beautifully describes as "the speed limit of your soul."[3] Listen for the rhythms of God's grace and live according to its cadence— easy, light, full of mercy.

For ways to safeguard yourself and maintain a healthy kind of self-denial, be sure that you're incorporating godly accountability into your life to provide objectivity—an outside source of authority like a coach, mentor or spiritual leader (to help balance our natural talent for self-delusion). Have a plan and strategy in place that is rooted in intimacy with God more than adherence to a set of regulations.

Are you prone to "rule-following" legalism? If so, in what areas of your life?

Consider one or more of the areas where you felt the need to incorporate Sabbath margin in your life as you've gone through this study. Do you think you could be prone to legalism in this area? Why or why not.

"No" Means Enough

Back to the Egyptians, Exodus 16:27 tells us that on the seventh day, some of the Israelites went out to try gathering manna, even though they had been specifically told not to. The result shouldn't have been shocking. As predicted, "They did not find any."

In what ways do you find yourself "gathering nothing" or spinning your wheels when God would have you stop and rest in Him?

In what areas do the benefits (or lack thereof) that you are receiving not outweigh your investment of time, energy, and effort?

Can you identify when the "gathering nothing" began?

How can you step back inside the margins to set aside the "seventh day" for God?

When we cannot put boundaries around certain areas of our lives and "resist the urge to continue," what does this tell us about how we view God's ability to protect and provide for us?

In Leviticus 25:4–6, God gave the Israelites on odd command. He told them to grant a Sabbath rest to their land every seven years. For six years in a row they could sow, plant, and harvest their crops, but in the seventh year, they were to refrain from working the soil.

> "Whatever the land produces during the Sabbath year can be food for you—for yourself, your male or female slave, and the hired hand or foreigner who stays with you" (v. 6).

What practical impact do you think observing the every-seven-year rest for the land would make . . .

on the farmland?

on the faith of the farmer?

on the farmer's family?

on the society in which they lived?

Read Leviticus 25:20–22 to see God's provision for the sabbatical years. How does this provision require faith?

How does the provision resemble other areas of your faith walk with Jesus?

Could you share a story of a time when you exercised faith, and God later fulfilled the promise of Leviticus 25 to you?

In the video message, I said:

{ "We have to know when we've worked enough, tried enough, gathered enough, purchased enough, said enough, stored enough, kept enough, created enough, produced enough, generated enough, consumed enough, labored enough, expended enough, spent enough. Somebody has got to say 'ENOUGH IS ENOUGH.'" }

Underline the phrase that most describes you.

What are some of the indicators that a person has reached the "enough" marker in his or her life?

In the areas where you most struggle, what are some personal indicators you can set in place that will help you detect when you are at a stopping place?

God used Sabbath to transform the minds of the Israelites from a slave mentality to one of a free people. He did it by commanding them to honor a Sabbath day—which was critical—but His primary purpose was to create in them a Sabbath heart. By being obedient to the law of the Sabbath in their actions (resisting the urge to continue), their hearts and minds would begin to cultivate a different perspective about their new relationship toward work and toward Yahweh.

Mark Buchanan describes this beautifully:

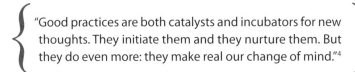

"Good practices are both catalysts and incubators for new thoughts. They initiate them and they nurture them. But they do even more: they make real our change of mind."[4]

As God's Spirit empowers you to honor the Sabbath by setting boundaries around areas of your life where you are prone to "slavery," you will likely find it difficult at first, painstaking even. And yet your heart and mind will be conformed in the process. Soon your desires and interests will follow suit.

In what areas has God already begun to transform your thinking in the time you've been doing this study?

Now, think more broadly. What additional areas has God significantly changed in you, not only recently, but since you first entered into relationship with Him?

In any of these areas, did you have to change your actions first in order to honor God, and then trust Him to progressively change your heart and attitude?

Take time here to celebrate God's accomplishments in your life. Think and make notes of the change He has made in you regarding the following areas:

1. your personal identity

2. your relationships

3. your sense of worth

4. your need to seek validation or approval

5. your relationship to work

Exodus 31:16 specifies that "the Israelites must observe the Sabbath, celebrating it throughout their generations as a perpetual covenant." Their adherence to this command, despite their feelings about it, would help them cultivate a heart and attitude of reverence to God for generations to come. Note particularly the word "celebrating." For the Jews, Shabbat, or Sabbath, is a great gift to be celebrated.

Judaism 101, an online encyclopedia of Judaism, says:

> "People who do not observe Shabbat think of it as a day filled with stifling restrictions, or as a day of prayer like the Christian Sabbath. But to those who observe Shabbat, it is a precious gift from G-d, a day of great joy eagerly awaited throughout the week, a time when we can set aside all of our weekday concerns and devote ourselves to higher pursuits. In Jewish literature, poetry and music, Shabbat is described as a bride or queen, as in the popular Shabbat hymn 'Lecha Dodi Likrat Kallah' (come, my beloved, to meet the [Sabbath] bride). It is said 'more than Israel has kept Shabbat, Shabbat has kept Israel.'"[5]

How differently would you greet Sabbath margin if you saw it as a beloved "bride or queen" coming to visit?

What do you think is meant by the phrase "more than Israel has kept Shabbat, Shabbat has kept Israel"?

In what ways can you foresee that keeping the Sabbath can actually end up keeping you?

This morning I read some of Exodus 24 with my sons where Moses is headed up Mount Sinai to meet with Yahweh. The boys looked at me so strangely when we got to verse16 because … well, I admit, I got overly giddy and excited.

> "The glory of the LORD dwelt on Mount Sinai, and the cloud covered it six days. And on the seventh day he called to Moses out of the midst of the cloud" (Ex. 24:16, ESV).

"… on the seventh day [Yahweh] called …"

I'm praying that the Lord brings all of the glory held in the arms of the "seventh day" to you and me. I'm asking, of course, that we'll see His presence and sense His favor in our every activity, every day of the week. But in those spaces and margins—those "seventh day" borders—that our "no's" create, may we hear the voice of God and experience nearness of fellowship with Him like never before.

YOUR BIG IDEAS …

WEEK 3
DOUBLE-PORTION
FRIDAY

SABBATH SET UP

Miracles.

Every single one of them is astounding, shocking, and overwhelming. Have you ever experienced one? An instance when God suspended the regular way that the universe functions to interject His activity?

Goodness gracious, I have.

I wish I was face to face with you right now so we could share our experiences (and some chocolate) with each other. What a conversation that would be—recounting the unusual activity of God in our lives. And actually, that's a good definition for a miracle that you and I can hang on to together: miracles are, by nature, unusual. They are unnatural occurrences that can only be accredited to the Divine.

If you can't put your finger on very many in your life and if, like me, you have a thirst for as many of them as God will graciously allow, I've got some good news for you: implementing Sabbath margin is one of the best places to begin.

Turns out, the Sabbath is a breeding ground for miracles.

One of the passages that you and I are studying, in fact—Exodus 16—records an unusual and subtle little miracle. In the desert when the Israelites gathered their fresh, new-every-morning manna, the Bible says that "some gathered a lot, some a little." But "when they measured it by quarts, the person who gathered a lot had no surplus, and the person who gathered a little had no shortage" (vv. 17–18). Like the multiplication of the loaves and fish (see Matt. 14:13-21), God made everyone's gathered manna just right for their need.

But on the sixth day when they got back from their morning manna ritual, they found that they'd "gathered twice as much food, four quarts apiece" (Ex. 16:22)—which would have been reasonable and understandable had the people spent twice as much time hunched over the desert sand that was laced with heaven's cornflakes that morning. Twice as much gathered for twice as much work. That makes sense, but that's not what happened. Each person, having spent just as much time and effort as normal, had raked in twice the result.

The people's leaders, shocked to see the robust bounty of their work, frantically reported to Moses the surprising outcome of the day's gleanings. But really, they shouldn't have been stunned at all. Can't you just picture Moses staring at them blankly, shaking his head and sighing as he replied, "This is what God was talking about ..." (v. 23, MSG).

Indeed, this is exactly what Yahweh had already said He would do for them. As they honored the seventh-day margin, God would give a double provision on the sixth-day in order to sustain the Israelites. And they wouldn't have to work overtime to reap it.

They wouldn't go hungry on the Sabbath, and they wouldn't need to make an extra trip to the wilderness "grocery store" to be sure of it. They didn't need to concern themselves with where their babies and elderly would find their nourishment. Yahweh had taken care of that. All they had to do was honor the Sabbath, and they could expect to receive His full supply. His double-portion supply.

God repeats this miracle of provision over and over in history and in the experience of His children even today. When we curtail our efforts and interests in obedience to the Spirit's conviction—resisting the gnawing sense of guilt or compulsion to keep pressing beyond the boundaries, beyond that which honors God—He will bless our obedience and sustain us. He will miraculously give twice the harvest, twice the fulfillment, twice the return, even though we haven't done anything more to garner it.

Unusual.

Double portions always are.

But sadly, I've often been unable to relish God's double-portion miracle for me. And I think you probably know the feeling. Because believing that doing less can somehow produce more requires a resilient faith. It takes an unshakable, concrete trust in God—the kind that won't topple even in an earthquake of doubt—to maintain the confidence that allows you to stop, even when everything in you and around you says keep going. Keep pushing. Keep gathering. Keep persisting.

That's hard for a slave.

That's why we're not surprised to see, in Exodus 16:20, that some of the newly freed slaves found a caveat for their weak faith in Yahweh. They decided to hoard God's provision, just in case this Sabbath thing didn't work the way they planned. We aren't told if they actually gathered more than what they needed, or if they deprived themselves in order to stretch what they had. Either way, they sought to store up manna beyond that which Yahweh had permitted. And the results were universally bad … and smelly.

God wanted them to trust in Him, not in their ability to provide for themselves. He wanted to give them a double-portion miracle so they could see what it felt like. But they couldn't experience it as long as their bent toward scarcity persisted. What's worse, they had missed out on the opportunity to see God do what He does best—be God.

This week, let's consider what we may be missing when we try to stockpile beyond that which is pleasing to God. In my study, I have become convinced that in our tendency to hoard, we unknowingly turn our backs on one of the greatest and most regular miracles our Father seeks to provide. Instead of having more, we end up impoverished, our lives scanty and meager, all because we disregard the foundation on which a double-portion miracle rests—the Sabbath.

SESSION 3: VIEWER GUIDE

SABBATH PRINCIPLES

I. Resist the urge to _____.

II. Remember what you _____ _____ _____.

Refuse to _____.

SESSION 3: GROUP QUESTIONS

✳ As a group, discuss the things in your life that were most difficult to put margin around last week.

✳ Were there any specific principles from your Bible study on the Sabbath that helped?

✳ Recall a time when you implemented margin in your life, despite a concern that there was still more to be accomplished, and saw a "double portion" of God's blessing.

✳ What is a scarcity mentality? In what areas of your life do you struggle with the fear of not having/being enough?

✳ Is there anyone in the group who can share a testimony of God's freedom in their lives? How has their perspective changed since then?

Video sessions available for purchase at *www.lifeway.com/breathe*

WEEK 3: GOD'S BUSINESS

THIS WEEK'S BIG IDEA:
Obey—God will take care of the rest.

When I was 24 years old, I met Anne Graham Lotz. When she spoke to me I fell slightly limp, with my mouth ajar, my eyes widened in reverence. Her words dripped with a sense of God's presence and approval that permeated every thread of our conversation. One thing she said to me has been tucked away in my heart from that day until now. "Priscilla, the Lord told me a long time ago that He would take care of my business if I would take care of His."

We have so much to tend to, don't we? Children and spouses and projects and endeavors fill our hours and our brain space. Somebody has to do them. Somebody has to fill in the gap of effort required to get from the beginning to the end. Most of the time, we assume that the individual responsible for it all should be us. It has to be us. Who else is going to do it?

BIG IDEA: Take care of God's business.
Let Him take care of yours.

Deep inside is there anything that you question whether or not God will take care of in your life? If so, what?

In what ways does this doubt stir insecurity in you?

How do you see these insecurities fleshed out in your actions? In your thoughts?

Prayerfully consider this: What, if anything, are you currently doing for yourself or for someone else that God is asking you to leave to Him?

What do you think a double-portion miracle from God could look like in this particular area of your life?

Many of the Israelites adopted a "Plan B." They kept some excess manna just in case God's supply didn't hold out.

In what ways have you preserved a "Plan B" in this area of your life?

What does this tell you about your level of trust and faith in God to "take care of your business"?

How might your inability to have confidence in God be keeping you from experiencing His activity in your life?

From the beginning of time until now, the primary purpose of God's miracles is to turn the hearts of His people to Himself. When God moves—when He makes His presence known in supernatural ways—the only appropriate reaction should be worship. Not to understand or analyze or explain, but simply to say, "Thank You." His goal is that we might more passionately seek out the Source of the miracle rather than the details of the miracle itself.

"The believing man does not claim to understand. He falls to his knees and whispers, 'God.' The man of earth kneels also, but not to worship. He kneels to examine, to search, to find the cause and the how of things." —A.W. Tozer[1]

When God does something unusual or unexplainable in your circumstances, which reaction most commonly describes you?

    □ worship God for the miracle
    □ investigate and rationalize the miracle

We'll explore this more next week, but I can't help but invite you to take a quick peek at Exodus 9, right now …

> "Then the LORD said to Moses, 'Go to Pharaoh and speak to him, "Thus says the LORD, the God of the Hebrews, 'Let My people go, that they may serve Me'"" (Ex. 9:1, NASB).

Turn in your own Bible to Exodus 8:20 and 10:3, and compare those verses with Exodus 9:1. Record the common thread running through these passages.

What's the main purpose Yahweh gives for Israel's freedom?

The purpose of Israel's liberty—and of everything else He would graciously provide during their wilderness journey (including the double-portion miracle)—was clear. They weren't being given freedom for freedom's sake, but so that they could be uninhibited in their pure devotion, service, and worship of Yahweh.

This makes the contrast between God's purposes and the methods of some of the Israelites very distinct. Those who did not have an appreciation for the Sabbath boundary that God had set were more consumed with conserving and accumulating manna than in honoring the manna-Giver. So, in essence, Yahweh's gifts became more important to them than Yahweh.

If you struggle with margin in a specific area of your life, what evidence do you see that your devotion to that person or thing has supplanted your consecration to God?

Remember When

One of the most important takeaways from Scripture is that freedom creates room for devotion to God. Within this liberty, Sabbath is an opportunity He has carved out for His people to stand in awe of His character, His power, and His handiwork. We can see this clearly in one of the specific principles from Deuteronomy 5. There are three. Record last week's below. Turn to page 46 if you need help.

Resist the urge to _____.

This week's principle is:

Remember what you used to be.

Even while Israel was enjoying freedom, why did they need to remember who they used to be?

How do you think "looking back" supports a sense of appreciation and gratitude?

We're all familiar with some Hollywood actors and overpaid sports stars who have become a bit spoiled and assume by their glamour and material excess that they are a little more special than everyone else. But then there are those rare celebrities who have somehow managed to keep it all in perspective. What you'll often hear in their humble explanation for why they stay so down-to-earth is something like, "I've never forgotten where I came from."

Those humble celebrities still remember the ordinary people they grew up with. They still remember the cheap rent and Ramen noodles that kept them alive before anyone discovered their talent. They still remember when their name merely showed up in random alphabetical order, not on concert tickets or movie trailers. They remember who they were, and it gives them a greater appreciation for who and where they are.

What role do you think remembering plays in authentic worship to God?

For the former slaves Moses was tasked with leading, an unobstructed view of their previous position would have made them more grateful. And more than that, it would also have given them perspective on their new way of living. The attributes and actions that described them in the past weren't supposed to define them now. The way they'd lived in Egypt was no longer to be their mode of operating.

They weren't slaves anymore. They were free. Free people shouldn't act the same way slaves do.

Take a closer look at a progression of statements I made during our video session together. For each group of statements, circle the one that most describes a transition you are making in this stage of your journey.

Slaves hoard.	Free people give.
Slaves live fearfully.	Free people live lovingly.
Slaves live with closed fists.	Free people live with open hands.
Slaves live from a posture of lack.	Free people live from a posture of abundance.
Slaves live from a stance of deficiency.	Free people live from a place of holy expectation.
Slaves never think they have enough.	Free people believe that whatever they don't have, God will graciously, miraculously, and abundantly give in His timing.
Slaves keep going.	Free people can willingly discipline themselves to stop.

In regard to the ones you circled, list some specific, practical ways you can begin to transition from the patterns of slavery to that of a free person. What are some things you can begin implementing right away?

Stingy from the Start

One of the most distinguishing characteristics of a slave mind-set is that it's rooted in scarcity and lack. Brutalized and brainwashed by their captors, the Hebrews rarely had enough of anything to meet their needs. The result of this kind of paltry living had made some of them hoarding, selfish vagabonds, unable to see the abundant goodness of Yahweh that was dripping from His hand directly into their dusty laps.

They were always afraid they wouldn't have enough, so letting go of any excess was unthinkable.

Honoring the Sabbath would require a migration out of the ideology of scarcity—a transformation that some of the Israelites could barely stand to make. Only a fresh look at Yahweh's abundance, of which they were now beneficiaries, could change the trajectory of their self-centered demise.

My three sons are each unique individuals—completely different from their brothers. One likes skinny jeans and leather jackets, and another would wear a sweat suit every day if I'd let him, no matter the occasion. One craves sweet chocolate and another salty popcorn. While one would rather socialize with friends, another could spend hours alone. They're just different.

But there is one way in which they are all similar—they each have a natural tendency toward selfishness. And the odd thing is, I didn't have to teach any of my kids not to share with their friends or to aggressively vie for first place in line. No formal training went into their tendency to swipe more cookies than they need or more breakfast bacon than they could ever eat, fearing there might not be any left later.

How in the world did this fear of lack—this dread of shortage—start dictating my children's actions? Gosh, we aren't perfect parents, but we've tried to make sure their needs have always been met and to train them to be generous and big-hearted toward others. Yet somehow, they just keep reverting back to a mind-set of fear—fear that there might not be enough.

This tells me that a scarcity mentality is hardwired into their DNA. I didn't have to teach it to them because Adam and Eve had already gifted it to them. Turns out, they have given it to you and me, too. We can easily be stingy with our time, energy, and money (among other things), all because of that slippery fall in the garden.

What do you have a tendency to hoard because you're worried you won't have enough?

Let's be clear, I'm not suggesting that we give away our time or money or energy without discretion. We need to be wise, of course. What I am proposing, however, is that our best option is never to retain what God is asking us to release. When God says, "Let go," we'll derive no benefit from clenching our fist tightly around the thing He is asking us to give. In fact, holding on will create an oozing sore of disease that will begin to eat away at the fabric of every area of our lives. Before we know it (and sadly, often when it's too late to do anything about it), we realize that by keeping more, we're actually left with less in the end.

It's the stunning irony of stinginess.

> "The world of the generous gets larger and larger; the world of the stingy gets smaller and smaller. The one who blesses others is abundantly blessed; those who help others are helped" (Prov. 11:24-25, MSG).

Read the above verse several times. It's OK. I'll wait.

In what way did keeping more manna actually amount to less for the Hebrews who hoarded in Exodus 16?

In what way did those who kept less actually have more than those who disobeyed God?

Is there any area of your life where you have seen your tendency toward excess eat away at other areas of your life?

Describe an area where you've watched your generosity create an increase your life.

What is God asking you to give away in obedience to Him?

What will make obedience to Him in this area of your life most difficult?

Think of someone you know or have heard of who is an example of Proverbs 11:24. Write her name in the margin. I love talking to people whose lives I admire. I shamelessly take notes right then and there so that I don't forget the wisdom she's sharing. If possible, make a point of talking soon to the person you listed, asking how she's seen the generosity principle operate in her life.

You can take notes of your conversation in the space provided below.

Scarcity Scares

Yes, scarcity scares. That's the simplest way to say it. It frightens you into disbelieving that God's provision is or can ever be sufficient. It exacerbates your selfish tendencies like a flare-up of poison ivy—itching and stinging and making you slather on the ointment of excess to soothe it. Except this kind of salve never quite works. It only makes things worse. It causes our lives to reek with the stench of things that are void of the blessing and favor of God.

Conversely, when we live within the boundaries that God's Spirit impresses on us, the things we do have will be accompanied by a divine nod of approval that will multiply their usefulness and our enjoyment of them.

Name any part of your life that has become distasteful to you recently.

In what way, if any, has excess played a role in this?

On the left side of the chart below, record some adjectives that describe how you used to feel about them. On the right side, record the emotions you feel when you think about them now. I'll give you an example of my own from my clothes closet.

How I used to feel:	How I feel now:
excited to go in and put an outfit together	overwhelmed and frustrated by the disorganization

As Mark Buchanan brilliantly and simply puts it, "Generous people generate things."[2] Generosity breeds. It produces. It creates. It fosters. It increases capacity and then rises up to meet the heightened outlook of its owner. Most of all, it releases you from the grip of terror that cages and keeps you from the double-portion miracle that God has stored up for you.

Scarcity scares? Yep. But generosity lets you let go.

And as you release *it*—the excess, the extra—God releases a miracle to you.

BIG IDEA: As you release it, God releases a miracle to you.

Have you ever thought about what the Israelite camp must have been like during this putrid period? It doesn't take much, you know, for the stench of something foul to permeate your entire house. A friend of mine had a little wayward critter that wandered into the rafters of her attic and died. They didn't know this, of course. All they knew was that an obnoxious scent was carrying through both stories of the house, even down into the basement, that couldn't be aired out for weeks. When they finally figured out what the culprit was—the decaying corpse of this one small creature—they were stunned.

Amazing how just one rotten egg or one unclean sewage line can leave a smell that careens through every single square foot. Then everything else under that roof falls prey to the unpleasantry. Eating, playing, working—it all becomes a bit nauseating.

Put enough houses (or tents) like this in one neighborhood, and a million or more at that, and you've got the worst episode of *Hoarders* you've ever seen in your life. Talk about disgusting. It only takes a little bit . . . to spoil everything else.

Look back at your chart. Have you experienced an inability to enjoy something in one area of your life because of overcommitment and overdoing in a entirely different area of your life? If so, which areas?

What have you learned from this?

Even as you do this lesson, do you detect the "scent of foulness" wafting into this very moment, making it unpleasant for you to do your study?

What about the people you love? How are those in your sphere of influence being affected by the "scent"?

What do you think you can do to restore beauty and balance in each of these areas of your life?

Again, who are some people you can solicit to help keep you accountable in this area of your life?

For you, what would becoming a more generous person look like in the following areas:

· in your relationship with others?

· in your relationship to things?

· in your relationship with God?

End this week's study with a prayer of surrender to your provider. Tell Him your fears or concerns about that which He is asking you to release. Then end your prayer using Anne Graham Lotz's statement as a guide: "Lord, I'll take care of Your business, and I'll trust You to take care of mine."

YOUR BIG IDEAS ...

WEEK 4

COMING INTO FOCUS

SABBATH SET UP

I enjoy stations like the Discovery Health Channel and the Discovery Channel. They always seem to air programs that capture my attention. Whether on a matter of biology or a detail of anatomy, stations like these always take an intriguing and informative perspective that keep millions of viewers glued to their television screens.

Recently, I ran across a program that showed a series of magic tricks—thrilling illusions that were difficult to figure out. Each one was more compelling than the last. I sat back in my chair bewildered. Every time I thought that I might've figured out one of the tricks, I was wrong.

Not even close.

I figured the producers must have been doing a series of fancy camera tricks to pull off the clever bait-and-switch act. But the show's host assured the viewing audience that nary a camera was involved in any deception. In fact, he said, there was no need for them to trick us . . . because we are actually masters at doing it to ourselves.

"Inattentional blindness," they call it. It's the foundation for every Houdini-like illusion crafted since the beginning of time. Magicians rely on it. The success of their show depends on it. Sometimes called "perceptual blind-ness," this phenomena is defined on one Internet encyclopedia as a human's "failure to notice a fully-visible, but unexpected object because attention is engaged on another task, event, or object."[1]

I think most humans fall prey to inattentional blindness regularly—not only when watching a skilled magician perform his show on stage. Happens to me all the time, actually.

Just the other day, in fact. I was driving home—basically on autopilot—completely disengaged from what I was doing, my mind on a million other things. I looked up, and all of a sudden, I was right at my driveway, needing to turn in. Already? I didn't even think I was anywhere close to home yet. Later, my neighbor called to asked me if I'd noticed the new humongous "For Sale" sign that had just gone up in front of one of the houses on our street. Nope. Hadn't seen it. Not because it wasn't in my line of sight but because I wasn't paying attention. What else might I have missed seeing along the way?

Has that ever happened to you?

How different from when I'm out walking or jogging down that same rural country road, paying full attention and marveling at the colors of wildflowers growing in a nearby field, locking eyes for a brief moment with a grazing horse or a cow, noticing a piece of lost change or a gum wrapper lying in the gravel on the shoulder—seeing everything, not missing a beat.

Inattentional blindness is the trick our own brains play on us—keeping us preoccupied with one thing while rendering us unaware and oblivious to another. So while we are concentrating somewhere else, another more critical action could be occurring within view, but without our conscious knowledge. Then, shocked and bewildered, we realize we missed something—or Someone—who really deserved our full attention.

This kind of blindness has nothing to do with vision and everything to do with attention.

It's all about focus.

The children of Israel had missed seeing Yahweh, even though He'd been directly in their field of vision for years. Overwhelmed with the many moving parts of their slavery in Egypt and then the distractions of wilderness travel, they had moved Him to the periphery of their attention. Even His gifts to them—this manna, for instance, delicate and delicious—had become more of a focus than Yahweh was.

They'd become consumed with the manna, hoarding it beyond the twenty-four hours they'd been licensed to keep it, seeking to gather it beyond the length of days they'd been instructed to collect it. They were distracted, preoccupied, and sidetracked from Yahweh's original intention for their liberty.

In setting out to research the Sabbath, I've discovered one of its primary goals; God gave us the Sabbath to refocus our attention—to cause us to bring to the center stage of our minds and hearts the Person who we have placed at the periphery far too long. Margin keeps us from marginalizing God.

SESSION 4: VIEWER GUIDE

SABBATH PRINCIPLES

I. Resist the urge to continue.

II. Remember what you used to be.

III. Recall what God has accomplished _____ _____ _____.

Rhema word: When the Holy Spirit takes a _____ message and applies it _____ to your life.

The Sabbath first comes up in the _____ _____.

SESSION 4: GROUP QUESTIONS

✳ Define *God's sovereignty*. How can a firm belief in it reframe your perspective on your current circumstances and upcoming decisions?

✳ In week 1, we discussed how God actually created Sabbath rest on the seventh day. Discuss any connections you may detect between that principle and the concept you learned today—that God made a declaration of His sovereignty on the seventh day.

✳ As a way to build each other's faith and encourage those who might be discouraged, take time to recall what the Lord has done on your behalf this week. How have you seen His presence, power, and activity in your circumstances recently?

✳ What are some other creative ways that you might be able to incorporate and apply the "14 Challenge" into your life?

Video sessions available for purchase at *www.lifeway.com/breathe*

WEEK 4: TOTAL RECALL

THIS WEEK'S BIG IDEA:
Margin keeps us from marginalizing God.

Reading through the children of Israel's experience with my own children has been a delightful undertaking this past year. The whole saga from the time of their enslavement through their wilderness travels is filled with enough shocking events that even three boys will lean in close to read, listen, and learn. I mean, with that whole Red Sea business and the thunder roaring on Mount Sinai, it's enough to make all of our eyes widen in suspense.

Without a doubt, our favorite part so far has been the ten plagues. Yahweh masterfully crafted ten miracles to bring immense difficulty to Pharaoh and his kingdom when he refused to release the Hebrews.

A few weeks ago, the boys and I had a blast reenacting the plague of hail. Tiny slivers of crushed ice from a fast-food restaurant, tossed lightly over their heads, might not depict the exact experience of those poor Egyptians being flattened by giant balls of ice, but it was enough to get my kids excited about the lesson, that's for sure. While my boys' favorite verse probably has something to do with frogs or diseased cattle, mine is tucked in Exodus 9 and reads like this:

> "Then the LORD said to Moses, 'Get up early in the morning and present yourself to Pharaoh. Tell him: This is what Yahweh, the God of the Hebrews says: Let My people go, so that they may worship Me. ... I have let you live for this purpose: to show you My power and to make My name known in all the earth'" (vv. 13,16).

Underline the two reasons Yahweh pinpointed as to why He allowed Pharaoh to continue to reign in Egypt.

God has always prioritized bringing glory to Himself, even if He needed to unleash the worst of plagues to do it. From the beginning of time until now, God's reasoning and purpose for allowing certain occurrences (or even creating them); His strategy for incorporating certain boundaries, or calling us to particular assignments, has always primarily reflected His intention to reveal His power and magnify His own name. More than anything. Even now, the Holy Spirit's main job in our lives is to bring glory to God—to position Him center stage in our experience (John 16:14). God clearly intends to situate Himself out of the margins and squarely into our center.

God's primary purpose constitutes a key part of the Sabbath principle— one that we will try to dig into a little more deeply this week.

But first, let's backtrack. Record the three Sabbath principles you've learned from our study:

Resist _____

Remember _____

Recall _____

Last week, we began to explore the fact that on the Sabbath, Israel was supposed to take time remembering the brutality of their slavery—a dismal and ominous assignment for sure. If this had been the full extent of their reminiscing, I suppose we could expect no other outcome but a serious case of depression. But this wasn't the end after all. For them or for us.

Thank You, Lord.

The whole point of remembering their slavery was to help them automatically become conscious of their current state of freedom. What a contrast! Relief was meant to sweep over their souls as they thought back to the shackles that had once tethered them to dusty walls and barren posts. A spring of gratitude would well up inside them because now they were liberated.

The Sabbath day was the occasion designed to give room for gratitude to swell into worship.

What might be some ways the Sabbath supported and encouraged the Israelites in worshiping Yahweh?

Sabbath was the predetermined space of time carved out so they could give God the honor and worship due to Him for setting them free. It was the segment divinely built into their new lives where they could refocus their attention on the real reason for their current state. Pausing from the regular rhythms of gathering manna, worrying about their supply, grumbling about their plight—all of these took a back seat on the Sabbath. During these hours, their frayed attention would be corralled into one singular focus—the only focus worth having—Yahweh.

Sabbath is designed to do the same for us.

For most Christians, the first part of their church service on Sunday morning is the only predetermined time they set aside for the worship of God. What other opportunities could you pinpoint on your calendar throughout the week to make intentional time for it?

Sabbath as Worship

Margin gives time for us to breath in and out—stilling ourselves in the presence of God and allowing all the things which have hustled our attention to be cast aside in favor of a purposeful look at our God. Sabbath dulls down the noisiness of our ever-pulsating activities, invites us to refocus our attention on His character, and all He has done for us. It helps us be thankful. It gives us space … to worship. It keeps us from squeezing the Giver out of the gift.

Pastor, author, and my dear ol' dad, Dr. Tony Evans, defines *worship* this way: recognizing God for who He is, what He has done, and what you are expecting Him to do.

Using the three elements of worship from this definition:

· Write down some characteristics God has revealed to you about Himself that you need to take time to recognize and acknowledge.

· List some things God has recently done on your behalf for which He deserves your worship.

· Consider the things you are expecting God to do. List them here and thank Him in advance.

Take a few moments to pause. Using the following verses, along with your answers to the questions you just considered, enter into a time of personal worship right now. Highlight portions of the passages that speak to you most, and then use them to construct your words of worship to God. You can do it audibly or in the quietness of your own heart. Either way, He'll hear and joyfully receive your praise.

"Praise the LORD! Let all that I am praise the LORD. I will praise the LORD as long as I live. I will sing praises to my God with my dying breath. Don't put your confidence in powerful people; there is no help for you there. When they breathe their last, they return to the earth, and all their plans die with them. But joyful are those who have the God of Israel as their helper, whose hope is in the LORD their God" (Ps. 146:1–5, NLT).

"Praise the LORD. How good it is to sing praises to our God, how pleasant and fitting to praise him! The LORD builds up Jerusalem; he gathers the exiles of Israel. He heals the brokenhearted and binds up their wounds. He determines the number of the stars and calls them each by name. Great is our Lord and mighty in power; his understanding has no limit. The LORD sustains the humble but casts the wicked to the ground" (Ps. 147:1–6, NIV).

Worship is not a style of music or a segment scheduled and labeled on a program. Sure, it can occur during those times, of course, but the occasion itself is not what worship is or ever will be. It is a perspective—an orientation of reverence—that leads to the act of saluting and honoring God. This kind of veneration requires a mental and spiritual focus that leaves little room for distraction.

In what ways do you think having margin in the things we accumulate can also foster authentic worship?

When you choose to have a Sabbath heart about your activities and possessions, you're doing more than just keeping yourself from living a stress-filled, clutter-laden life. You are also honoring God's purpose by setting aside space and time to foster holy intimacy. The break we take from the regular pattern of our lives in any area gives us occasion to see Yahweh clearly without the distraction and distortion of excess.

Psalm 92 is a song of worship for the Sabbath day. Read the Psalm that follows, and highlight any benefits God grants His people. Use the extra space beside the verses to record any insights the Lord brings to your mind. I'd also like to challenge you to memorize this passage. If you take on two verses a day, you'll have it down in just a little more than a week.

¹"It is good to praise Yahweh,
   to sing praise to Your name, Most High,
²to declare Your faithful love in the morning
   and Your faithfulness at night,
³with a ten-stringed harp
   and the music of a lyre.
⁴For You have made me rejoice, LORD,
   by what You have done;
   I will shout for joy
   because of the works of Your hands.
⁵How magnificent are Your works, LORD,
   how profound Your thoughts!
⁶A stupid person does not know,
   a fool does not understand this:
⁷though the wicked sprout like grass
   and all evildoers flourish,
   they will be eternally destroyed.
⁸But You, LORD, are exalted forever.
⁹For indeed, LORD, Your enemies—
   indeed, Your enemies will perish;
   all evildoers will be scattered.
¹⁰You have lifted up my horn
   like that of a wild ox;
   I have been anointed with oil.
¹¹My eyes look down on my enemies;
   my ears hear evildoers

when they attack me.
¹²The righteous thrive like a palm tree
and grow like a cedar tree in Lebanon.
¹³Planted in the house of the LORD,
they thrive in the courts of our God.
¹⁴They will still bear fruit in old age,
healthy and green,
¹⁵to declare: "The LORD is just;
He is my rock,
and there is no unrighteousness
in Him" (Ps. 92).

What did you notice regarding the benefits of each of the following?

rejoicing?

wisdom?

protection?

provision?

Consider the connection between the following passages. Underline any you detect.

> "Take delight in the LORD, and He will give you your heart's desires" (Ps. 37:4).

> "If you ... call the Sabbath a delight and the holy day of the LORD honorable; if you honor it, not going your own ways ... then you shall take delight in the LORD, and I will make you ride on the heights of the earth; I will feed you with the heritage of Jacob your father" (Isa. 58:13-14, ESV).

Fill in the blanks: The psalm commands us to delight in the _____. The Isaiah passage says to delight in the _____ and then you will delight in _____ as a result.

How might considering the Sabbath a "delight" lead to or enhance delighting in the Lord?

If honoring Sabbath margins in your life can promote a healthy relationship with the Lord, consider the opposite effect that neglecting it may have. On a recent trip to my father's childhood neighborhood in Maryland, I saw something that may help you to think about this possibility. The community, once safe and docile, is now riddled with the damage of drug infestation and crime. Row homes that lined one particular street were boarded up, tattooed with graffiti and crawling with shifty drifters. Daddy explained that it hadn't always been that way, but one unprotected, neglected home had spread like a cancer down the block. One broken window here, one vandalized residence there, one unaddressed graffiti post over there, had led to the deplorable conditions on the rest of the street.

This is the "broken window theory"—an idea that comes from the world of law enforcement and basically says if a building is left vacant in a community and someone breaks some of its windows, one of two things follow: either a) the unrepaired windows will invite and encourage vandalism and crime, or b) the windows can be quickly repaired, and the downward spiral of deplorable conditions will be curtailed. The driving philosophy behind this theory is that quick prosecution of minor crime decreases major crime.

Just as in the broken window theory, how do you think neglecting the Sabbath—space and time to honor God—might invite the growth of other sin in our lives?

How might honoring Sabbath margin encourage the growth of righteousness in other areas of life?

Sovereignty and Sabbath

In the video message, I mentioned an author and scholar by the name of Sandra Richter. She has written one of my favorite books, *The Epic of Eden*. I've read it three times and fully intend to read it again soon. I've marked it up with notes and underlinings on every one of her wisdom-rich pages.

One of the seminal ways the Lord began to cement the importance of Sabbath in my heart was through her explanation of the Sabbath day's placement in the creation story.

Remember, Yahweh designed each day's events strategically to make a statement of sovereignty. His purpose was to point to His ultimate control and authority over all that exists—including your life and mine.

I want us to dig our hands and hearts more deeply into this concept together. Here is the progression of creation:

DAY 1   DAY AND NIGHT

DAY2   HEAVENS AND OCEANS

DAY 3   LAND AND VEGETATION

DAY 4   SUN AND MOON

DAY 5   BIRDS AND FISH

DAY 6A   LAND ANIMALS

DAY 6B   MAN AND WOMAN

DAY 7   GOD'S SABBATH

Use the information from the previous page to complete the diagram. Take a moment and fill it in, then I'll meet you back here.

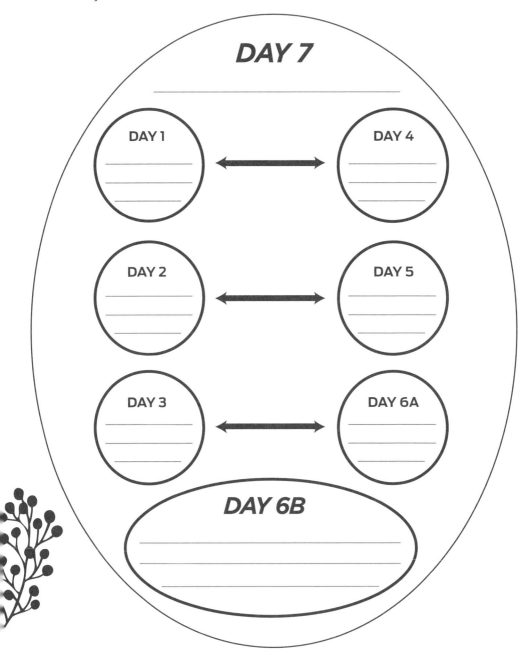

DAY 7

DAY 1

DAY 4

DAY 2

DAY 5

DAY 3

DAY 6A

DAY 6B

Here is a quote from Old Testament scholar Meredith Kline that helps us understand the progression of creation even more clearly:

"A hierarchical pattern of dominion can be traced through the creational record, a pattern of ascending consecration with the Sabbath as its capstone. Within the first three day-frames is described the origin of three vast spheres over which rule is to be exercised. Then in day-frames four through six the rulers of each of these spheres is presented in proper turn, each arising at the divine behest and ruling by divine appointment. But the rising chain of command does not stop with the six days; it ascends to the seventh day, to the supreme dominion of him who is Lord of the Sabbath."[2]

Underline the last sentence of the quote above, and then take a few moments to read it slowly, prayerfully considering its meaning.

How would you describe the "rising chain of command" shown in the pattern of creation?

What does the fact that it did not stop at the sixth day tell us about the meaning and importance of the seventh?

Keeping in mind the "chain of command," if there had been an eighth or ninth day of creation, what would this have done to the statement made on the seventh?

Now, using your thoughts from the previous questions, rewrite the highlighted phrase from Kline's quote in your own words.

In creation, God didn't take a seventh-day Sabbath because He was exhausted from creating the world. When you think about it, He didn't actually expend that much energy. He spoke, His words took shape, and He called it good. Easy . . . (to Him). But in taking the Sabbath, He was making a statement about His supreme authority and sovereignty over all.

BIG IDEA: The Sabbath is a statement about God's sovereignty.

Even though God gave Adam and Eve dominion over the garden, He was still in ultimate authority over it and them. They were its managers, but He was the owner. So He had every right to withhold that one forbidden tree from them, creating a boundary for the first two humans. It was His garden. And when they chose to step beyond that boundary and into the margin He'd commanded them not to enter, they rebelled against the most important declaration He'd made in the entire creation process: I Am Sovereign.

Sovereignty means that God has all power, is the supreme ruler over all, and has the absolute right to do all things according to His own good pleasure.

What role might pride have played in Adam and Eve's decision?

When we step into the margins that are supposed to be set aside at God's bidding, we do exactly what the first couple did. We pridefully usurp the authority of God. Conversely, when we honor God's margins and the boundaries He has instituted, we endorse His authority, express our continued need for Him, invite His favor in our lives, and bring honor to His name.

Think back to the areas you ranked overwhelming in your life. (It was at the beginning of our study on p. 11.) What part does pride play in your struggle with margin in this area?

Now, write these problem areas next to the words "God's Sabbath" on the creation chart. As you do, consider how a commitment to implementing Sabbath in these areas will enable you to honor and affirm your commitment to God's sovereignty. Write only the ones that you are honestly planning to yield to Him right now. You can add others later as you continue to grow in this area.

As you honor Sabbath margin in these areas, what kind of statement will you be able to make about God's sovereignty ...

to yourself?

to others in your sphere of influence?

How else might showing more reverence to God's sovereignty create a beneficial, ripple effect in other areas of your life?

How might showing more reverence for God's sovereignty affect the people in your sphere of influence?

If you have children (or young people in your life whom you influence), what are some of the ways you expect they might be affected by seeing you honor God's margin in your life?

How do you hope their lives might look different than your own in the area of margin and boundaries as they mature?

What are some creative ways that you can teach them to honor God's sovereignty?

Sabbath Blessings

When Adam and Eve aligned themselves beneath the sovereignty of God, they experienced no worry, selfishness, or shame. They were free from violence, abuse, lies, and discord. They had no fear or inclination to be unproductive. And best of all, they felt no friction in their relationship with their Creator. They received His blessing and favor upon all of their endeavors. But once they circumvented God's authority, all of the benefits He'd given them became fleeting. They now had to work harder in every area of their lives, but they achieved much less.

Since God has always honored humility, what can you expect to receive from Him as you forgo pride and submit to His boundaries? (Some verses that might help with your answer include 2 Chronicles 12:7; Proverbs 11:2; James 4:6; and 1 Peter 5:6.)

When God is honored, when His authority is kept in proper perspective, all the blessing and favor He intends to give His children become a part of their experience. But when we seek to be our own sovereign ruler, we (like Adam and Eve) will find that we're working harder for fewer, less satisfying results.

Read this telling excerpt from Richard Swenson's best-selling book, *Margin/The Overload Syndrome.* Underline the portions that speak most directly to you.

{ "God does not have to depend on human exhaustion to get His work done. God is not so desperate for resources to accomplish His purposes that we have to abandon the raising of our children in order to accommodate Him. God is not so despairing of where to turn next that He has to ask us to go without sleep five nights in a row. Chronic overloading is not a spiritual prerequisite for authentic Christianity. Quite the contrary, overloading is often what we do when we forget who God is."[3] }

As we conclude our study, please notice the word *chronic* in Swenson's quote. Tucked inside its meaning is a bit of hope for us any time we find ourselves getting off track, sucked back into the whirlwind of busyness and excess. Let's think about it for just a second.

Look in the dictionary or thesaurus and flesh out the meaning of the term *chronic*. List some synonyms for it below.

Now, rewrite the following sentence in your own words: "Chronic overloading is not a spiritual prerequisite for authentic Christianity."

A situation that is chronic is habitual and long lasting. It's not a short-term condition resulting from a new set of circumstances that has been introduced into our lives. The word *chronic* implies a routine that's become ingrained over time into our mind-set and our usual way of living. It's a road we are deliberately traveling without awareness or interest of the off-ramps we're passing along the way.

We do experience other seasons that are just that—seasons. Short-term periods. Temporary phases that bring heavier demands on our time and energy than others. In every life there will come times that require us to fill our spaces and margins beyond those limits by which we have sought to abide. Maybe this study has met you during one of those stages.

When this happens (and it will), don't get discouraged or off-track from your intention. Just refocus, reprioritize, and get back in step as you are able. And don't allow yourself to be overcome with a sense of guilt or condemnation. Remember: just as chronic overloading doesn't cause us to accumulate brownie points with God, short-lived overcrowding doesn't garner His disapproval. Your Sabbath heart will be seen and known by God even when your Sabbath margins are blurred and smudged by reality.

God will know.

He will know your desire to honor His sovereignty, and He will honor it with the nearness of His presence, the abundance of His grace, and the blessing of His favor upon all that you put your hands to do.

So press on, Sister—even if it's just fourteen minutes at a time. Press on in freedom … in faith … and in the fullness of God.

YOUR BIG IDEAS ...

SESSION 5: VIEWER GUIDE

✱ How might considering the Sabbath a "delight" lead to or enhance delighting in the Lord?

✱ How do you think neglecting the Sabbath might invite the growth of other sin in our lives? How might honoring Sabbath margin encourage the growth of righteousness in other areas of life?

✱ What part do you think pride plays in your struggle with the areas you've identified as potentially overwhelming? (p. 105)

✱ How did you rewrite the sentence, "Chronic overloading is not a spiritual prerequisite for authentic Christianity"? What insights did you have from that statement?

✱ What big ideas do you plan to take away from this study?

Video sessions available for purchase at *www.lifeway.com/breathe*

ENDNOTES

WEEK 1

1. Harriet Tubman, as quoted in "Free Blacks in the United States, 1619 to 1863," by Alonford James Robinson, Jr., *Africana: The Encyclopedia of the African and African American Experience,* Kwame Anthony Appiah and Henry Louis Gates Jr., Eds. (New York: Basic Civitas Books, 1999), 784.

2. Abraham Joshua Heschel with Susannah Heschel, *The Sabbath: Its Meaning for Modern Man* (New York: Farrar, Straus, Giroux, 1951), 10.

3. Ibid., Heschel, 10-11.

4. Brad Lomenick, "Make Time for Margin," Blog: Brad Lomenick On the Journey. Posted Feb. 25, 2013. Accessed June 12, 2014. Available online: *www.bradlomenick.com.*

5. Sandra L. Richter, *The Epic of Eden: A Christian Entry into the Old Testament* (Downers Grove, IL: InterVarsity Press, 2008), 105.

6. Barbara Brown Taylor, "Divine Subtraction," *The Christian Century,* Nov. 3, 1999. Available online: *www.christiancentury.org.*

7. Eugene H. Peterson, *Working the Angles* (Grand Rapids: Wm B. Eerdmans Publishing Co., 1987), 73.

WEEK 2

1. James Chastek, "Our ecclesiastical, social, and cultural abandonment of self-denial," Blog: Just Thomism. Posted July 13, 2010. Accessed June 18, 2014. Available online: *https://thomism.wordpress.com.*

2. Ibid.

3. Richard A. Swenson, *Margin/The Overload Syndrome* (Colorado Springs, CO: NavPress, 1998), 125.

4. Mark Buchanan, *The Rest of God: Restoring Your Soul by Restoring Sabbath* (Nashville, TN: Thomas Nelson, 2006), 6-7.

5. Tracey R. Rich, "Shabbat," Judaism 101. Accessed June 11, 2014. Available online: *www.jewfaq.org.*

WEEK 3

1. A. W. Tozer, *The Pursuit of God* (CreateSpace Independent Publishing Platform, 2013), 45.

2. Ibid., Buchanan, 83.

WEEK 4

1. Daniel J. Simons, "Inattentional blindness," Scholarpedia, (2007). Available online: *www.scholarpedia.org.*

2. Meredith G. Kline, *Kingdom Prologue I* (Meredith G. Kline, 1986), 30; as it appears in *The Epic of Eden* by Sandra Richter.

3. Ibid., Swenson, 36.

IDEAS FOR SMALL GROUPS

While you can complete this study as a personal effort, one of the best ways you can benefit is to get involved in a meaningful small group. Maybe you are already in a group but want to connect more deeply. Maybe you need to start a small group in your neighborhood, at your church, or with women you know. Either way, here are nine ways to cultivate a sacred and special group that will strengthen your relationship with Christ.

1. Be small. A large group of women can be fun, but it's not always best relationally. Don't be exclusive, but keep your small group small. This encourages everyone to have a voice in the discussion and fosters an atmosphere for true connection. You don't want someone to feel invisible in a big crowd. Plus, smaller groups feel safer. People will be more open than they would in front of lots of strangers. Consider agreeing on a reasonable number (give or take) so that your group doesn't get too big.

2. Be choosy. Discuss new study ideas as a group, and select things that resonate with the women collectively.

3. Be responsible. Don't let one or two people shoulder the responsibility for the entire group. Everyone can pitch in and should contribute. Have a sign-up sheet to rotate bringing snacks. Let women take turns leading the discussion. Encourage everyone to say the closing prayer once in a while.

4. Be consistent. Meet regularly at the same time and location. Ask women to commit to showing up. If a woman doesn't think she will be able to make it to most sessions, encourage her to wait until your next study begins. No one is taking roll and checking off a list, but having women consistently show up creates an environment of trust. Also be mindful to end on time. Everyone has had to make an effort to fit this study into their schedules. Close when you said you would so women can get back to their pets, relieve the babysitter, get in bed early, or do whatever they have planned with that time.

5. Be vulnerable. No one wants to be a part of a group where they feel like they are the only one with problems (and, therefore, won't share them). Set aside time for everyone to tell their stories—the milestones that have brought them to where they are today. No one's life is perfect, and realizing that everyone in the room has had bumps along the road is so refreshing. And the more vulnerable you are, the more others will open up.

6. Be trustworthy. Women need to be fully confident that this group is a safe place and what they say will not be repeated or discussed outside of their presence. Accept people exactly where they are without judgment. When women do share openly, remember that they aren't asking to be fixed. Many times the best thing to do is just listen. Wait to be asked for advice. And if you are asked, speak the truth in love and be open to the fact that what works for you might not work for another.

7. Be prayerful. Pray with and for each other. Set aside time at the end of each meeting for everyone to share a personal prayer request. This is not a request for your coworker's grandmother's sick cat. This is an opportunity to share real things about yourself. If fitting this into the allotted time won't work, have everyone write down their requests and exchange with someone they can pray for throughout the week.

8. Be hungry. Jesus regularly ate with His disciples, and we should follow His lead! Plan a meal between studies just to be together. Talk about day-to-day life, what study you'd like to do next, little known facts about each other, or all of the above.

9. Be together. Once a year, plan a retreat with these women you've grown so close to. A weekend away from your busy lives will allow you to make memories and bond like the sisters in Christ you are.

Breathe
Group Leader Guide

The following suggestions can give you ideas for leading a *Breathe* group. Always take the suggestions as a place to start, but pray and complete your own study. The point of a group study is to support each other as you apply God's Word to your lives. Since every group is different, and since you have unique strengths and weaknesses, combine these suggestions with your creativity to find the best way to conduct a group. We have supplied you with more ideas and questions than your group can possibly use. Select those you believe will be helpful. Remember that often the Holy Spirit will lead the group to minister to each other in ways this guide could never anticipate. Exercise the freedom to follow the Spirit's leadership while keeping the group on task.

Since this study is different from some of Priscilla's other studies, make sure your group members have clarity on how they should use it. Let them know that their book is more of a journal than the traditional Bible study workbook. Each week's material will read like a book with room for them to write their responses and thoughts. The intention is not for them to "finish" but to digest what they are processing. Encourage them to stop at any point that they read a question, Bible verse, or paragraph that stirs conviction so that they can ponder and pray through the things that God is doing in their hearts.

Promoting the Group Study

Promote the group through church bulletin announcements, posters, community announcements, social media, and personal invitation. You will want to enlist an adequate number of small group leaders to provide a discussion group for every group of no more than twelve women. The large group can view the video sessions together but will need to break into smaller groups to discuss. At *www.lifeway.com/breathe* you will find downloadable promotion helps.

A Five-Week Group Plan

Because *Breathe* came out of the final Deeper Still Live event, it's a different format than you may have done with other studies. You may custom design the group experience to fit the needs of your group and church. The suggested plan here is for a five-session group experience or as a retreat. In this format the group will work as follows:

Session 1: Get acquainted, distribute books, and watch the video for session 1. During the week, members will use the questions and journal for week 1.

Session 2: Discuss the questions and journal from week 1. Then view video for session 2. During the week, members will use the questions and journal for week 2.

Session 3: Discuss the questions and journal from week 2. Then view the video for session 3. During the week, members will use the questions and journal for week 3.

Session 4: Discuss the questions and journal from week 3. Then view the video for session 4. During the week, members will use the questions and journal for week 4.

Session 5: Discuss the questions and journal from week 4. Then conclude the group. Consider ending with a fellowship meal and plan future ministry with outreach to other women.

Each week before your group session:

View the video session and complete your viewer guide. Make notes of anything your group may need to further clarify. After the introductory week, complete the questions in the study guide for the next discussion and select those you believe your group will want to discuss. This means you will be completing week 1 questions and journal while previewing week 2 video, and so forth.

Draw from the suggestions given in the following leader guide. Pray about what goals the session most needs to meet, and plan your lesson to accomplish those goals. You may wish to make up your own group discussion sheet to give group members. Members will relax into the experience more if they know where they are going.

Remain open to the Spirit's leadership. Sometimes a group member will come with a concern or question that will result in a wonderful group experience that will bless the entire group. Other times you may need to avoid letting someone hijack the group into side issues. Experience and reliance on the Spirit will help you to know the difference. You will probably find that you will never get it right every time. If the group members are getting into the material, praying, and studying Scripture, your leadership will bear fruit.

Remember the real goal of the study. We need to understand, appreciate, and apply the Bible's teaching about Sabbath to our lives. If the women in the group make progress toward establishing a God-margin in their schedules and living spaces, the group will have been a great success. God may lead each woman in the group to establish that margin in a different way. The goal of the group is progress, not perfection, in reclaiming God's gift and command of Sabbath.

Session 1
THE FREEDOM OF THE SABBATH

1. Welcome the women to the group. You may want to plan activities to get acquainted as is appropriate for your group.

2. Stress the importance of trust in the group. Though this is not a support group, members must commit to confidentiality to establish trust. You may want to develop a group covenant together. Emphasize that in no case does any member have to share, nor should they share anything that would harm themselves or others. We will be learning that God does not expect us to expose ourselves without discretion. Stress that each member must remain responsible to God alone regarding how they follow His teaching about Sabbath.

3. Watch the first session video, complete the viewer guides, and then discuss.

4. Encourage the women to spend some time this week thinking and praying about the topic. The material in this study guide/journal will provide them some helps for exploring the concepts in the study.

5. Pray together and dismiss.

Session 2
THE FREEDOM OF THE SABBATH/ STOPS ALONG THE SABBATH JOURNEY

1. Welcome the group.

2. Ask what insights members have encountered in their study this week. Lead the discussion of week 1 questions. You may draw from the following suggested questions, or if the women volunteer insights, simply guide the sharing.

Suggested Discussion Starters/Questions

- How would you explain the idea that recognition is a prerequisite to liberation? What example would you use from your life of how God brought recognition before liberating you in some area?

- What three areas did you identify that present the greatest danger for you of becoming enslaved? (p. 11)

- How do you respond to Abraham Heschel's idea that rest involved a genuine act of creation? How would you share the idea with a child or younger believer? (pp. 14-16)

- Could you describe a time when you saw rest created in your life as a result of exercising Sabbath margin in an area? (pp. 16-17)

- Why do you suppose we tend to view Sabbath space from a negative perspective? (p. 16)

- Have you identified areas of your life that have suffered as a result of neglecting God's command to stop and practice tranquility?

- How does the fear of being perceived as weak or lazy impact your practice of Sabbath margin? (p. 21)

- What deep-seated reasons did you identify for why we tend to think busier lives are better? (pp. 22-23)